"Did You Sa[y...]
Other True St[ories]

by Rhea Beth Compton

Dedication

This book is lovingly dedicated to the memory of my Mother, Arlene Compton, my late brother Lonnie, my grandparents, Loren and Della Morgan, and to those brave men and women I worked with, who gave their all. I want their spirits to know that their sacrifices are remembered and appreciated.

FOREWORD

As Rhea "Beth" Compton recounts the true tales of her time as a police dispatcher, this book is definitely an interesting look into the day by day insanity that many of our nation's emergency dispatchers have to deal with. It also highlights the unique relationship between dispatchers and the police officers that they work with. Prepare to laugh till your sides hurt as you go through these stories, and learn of the top secret inter-planetary peace treaty with aliens and the sky police, and find your true love in a tree! But watch out for those Arizona alligators; they are vicious. You definitely do not want to be the target of one of her pranks; just ask any one of her officers, or the criminals that crossed her. She is certainly a whirlwind force to be reckoned with, as the book shows all too well. When it comes down to the grind, you have to be a little crazy to deal with this sort of crazy. These stories are absurd, insane, scandalous, shocking, and I loved every one of them! Sit back, read this book and enjoy.

Wesley R. Boyett
Youngtown, Arizona
August 25, 2017

Acknowledgments

For my son Jim, who has been the absolute love of my life since he was born.

My brother, Chuck.

To my friends Linda Headrick, Karen Becker, Sara Alvarez, Elizabeth Cardenas, Lela Mara, Carrie Baker, Vicki Poole, Susan Paris, Pilar Gomez, Randi Borgnis, Patricia Hagen, Danetta Phillips, and Claudia Davis, for their constant encouragement.

And especially to (Retired) Maricopa County Sheriff Joe Arpaio, who always had faith in me, and never hesitated to say so.

Credits

Managing Editor: Elisheva Zimmerman,
eggcellentediting@yahoo.com

Associate Editor: James Compton,
eggcellentediting@yahoo.com

Cover Design by Ed Saenz
http://edsaenz.folio.com,
and dgital.ed@gmail.com

A Word From The Author

When this book was first published, it was the first of it's kind. It was the first to actually poke fun at the crazy capers that make up so much a part of police work.

I spent the better part of two decades in police work. I handled everything from homicides, to firebombs, house fires, accidents and the deaths of friends who gave their absolute all to the job. I had studied many years in college in order to be ready for what I thought would be a career as a police officer. Because of my poor eyesight, that was not to be, so I ended up as a 911 operator.

What I was unprepared for was the absolute lunacy that accompanied each and every shift, as I fielded numerous calls from people in "peril" of a questionable nature. I was constantly amazed and aggravated over the fact that the system was often cluttered up by the stupid nature of those that abuse the system. A woman calls to ask where to buy a ceiling fan because with the hot July temperatures, she "felt" like it was an emergency. The idiots who use the 911 system for "information" because they're too lazy to look up the non-emergency number. There were so many times I simply wondered where the hell was Captain Kirk when I needed him to tell

Scotty to beam me up and get me out of there!

Enjoy the following stories. All of them are true. But please, learn to use the system the way it was intended. It isn't for jokes, or stupid questions. It was meant to save lives.

Section One: It's Not Mr. Rogers' Neighborhood!

Neighbor Problems

It was usually very quiet on Saturday mornings. But that wasn't the case on this particular Saturday. The 911 line rang at 10 o'clock and the man on the other end was furious. He was demanding to speak to an officer immediately. "What is the problem, sir?" I asked.

"It's these damned Mexican neighbors!" he fumed.

"What exactly are they doing?" I asked, trying to get more information.

"They're being *Mexicans*!" he yelled.

Rolling my eyes, I said, "Sir, you will have to be more specific. There's no law against being Mexican, especially here in the desert southwest. Now," I prompted, "tell me what they are *doing*?"

"Will you just send a cop out here?" he screamed. "And I want a white cop, not that *black* one you've got driving around town!"

Raising my eyebrow, I bit my tongue and forced myself to keep my voice even. Then I decided to have some fun with this idiot. "Well, sir," I said, "I have Officer Smith on duty right now"

"Is he black?" the man demanded.

"Oh no, sir," I answered truthfully. "Officer

Smith is *not* black."

"Fine," he said. "You send him and I'll tell him what my problem is!" He slammed down the phone.

I forced myself to keep from laughing as I was dispatching the call. There were two things I had "forgotten" to tell the complainant. Officer Smith was a woman. And her maiden name was Lopez! This was going to be fun!

I called her on the radio, and using the exaggerated Mexican accent that I usually reserved for teasing her, I said, "Hey, you gotta see the man about *problemas* with his neighbors!"

She responded in kind. "Hey what kinda *problemas*?"

"He says they're being *Mexicans!*" I said gleefully!

Oh," she said, "I gotcha! I take care of that one right now, yes ma'am!"

"10-4 ma'am," I said and then started laughing in my seat. There was an officer in the station doing paperwork. Lee gave me a stern look, and said, "I can't believe you just did that!"

Trying my best (and failing!) to look innocent, I said, "Are you talking to *moi*?" Lee just shook his head and grinned. His report forgotten, he pulled up a chair in dispatch, following the incident with interest!

Officer Smith drove to the address, parked across the street from the residences and watched for a few minutes. The *offending* Mexicans were setting up their yard for a barbecue. Two small kids were in the yard, playing with a ball; the husband (who happened to be active duty in the US Air Force) was firing up the grill, while his wife (who was *not* Mexican) was setting up the tables and tablecloths. Officer Smith went first to them to ask what was going on.

The Airman told her that the next-door neighbor came running out of his house, calling them a bunch of *wetbacks,* and told him to get his "brown ass" back to Mexico. He was ranting and screaming and cussing at his children. The Airman told him to get off of his property before he punched his lights out, and not so gently escorted the man off his property.

Officer Smith asked if he wanted to press charges against the neighbor for disorderly conduct. The Airman said no, that he would handle any further problems. Officer Smith gave him her card and told him to call her if the man came back.

Then she went next door.

The complainant obviously hadn't been expecting to see a petite Mexican American woman at his door in police uniform. Smith, being the sarcastic type of person she could be, put on an accent so thick that she could barely be understood and yelled loud enough to be heard by anyone in the vicinity, "Hey you having *problemas* with those *estupido* Mexicans? You tell me what those *estupido* Mexicans are doing and I go tell them *estupido* Mexicans not to be so *estupido*!"

He slammed the door in her face.

When he called back on the 911 line, he was furious! "I told you not to send me a damned Mexican!" he screamed.

"No you didn't," I yelled back, while bouncing up and down in my chair. "You said don't send the *black* guy!" I was seriously having fun with this one!

He continued to scream, "Well I want a *white* cop and I want him right now!"

"I don't know what to tell you," I said. "We don't have a white cop in stock right now. However," I said, in my attempt to be customer service oriented, "we do have a *Jewish* one coming on duty at 1700 hours. That's 5 PM your time," I added helpfully.

"I know what time that is," he yelled, "and I don't want no damned Jew!"

I was beginning to tire of this guy, so I said, "Then you'll have to wait until 2100 hours when Officer Schultz comes on duty. However," I cautioned, "he's a fluent Spanish Speaker and has a Chinese girlfriend, so I don't think he's going to care very much."

The man slammed down the phone and tried to call the Sheriff's Office. They were even less sympathetic to his plight than I was, and told him to call us back. I never heard from him again.

The Master Race? Really?

At the time I dispatched calls for Surprise Police Department, the city was largely an Hispanic community. Fairly small, it was a close knit community with more than their share of gangs and drugs. It was mostly a very poor area. It wasn't the large metropolis that it is today.

Which is why I was so shocked when my 911 lines were lighting up that Friday night with the angry, hysterical calls.

There were a couple of men who had come to the area, spouting "White Power" and looking for recruits for their Neo Nazi cause. The members of the community were very offended and getting angrier by the minute. I'm still surprised that anyone bothered to even call the police. One woman explained it as clearly as possible when she said, "My son is out there and he's on probation. I don't want him going back to jail over these idiots!" That made sense to me.

I dispatched the troops to the area. I had two Mexican officers, one black cop and a Jewish officer that responded. I wouldn't allow Schultz to go. He was a little put out and called me on the phone. "Why can't I go see the Nazis?" he demanded in his deep baritone voice.

"You're too white, Nick," I said. "I don't want them thinking they can bond with you in any way. And," I added gleefully, "I want them to *know* that they owe their lives to two Mexicans, a black and a Jew!" He laughed and told me I had an evil mind. Then he said he would be nearby in case help was needed.

The other guys knew exactly what I was doing. They arrived to an angry mob scene that was rapidly turning ugly. The crowd parted for the officers, but they were ready to attack.

My boys went to work immediately. Tony and Miguel started speaking with such thick accents that I could barely understand them on the radio. The black officer, Mark, went into deep, down home Southern mode, even going so far as to call Tony (the sergeant on scene) "*Massah.*" And Erik, my Jewish officer, "*oy vey*'d" everything, from their rhetoric to the fact that they were dropping loads in their underwear. (I found out later that he even kept a *kippa* in his car for just such emergencies, and was wearing it when he arrived on the scene!) Even the crowd was starting to calm down, and were laughing at the situation. My cops had to escort the idiots to the town line to make sure they made it out of town alive. Tony, ever so helpful, said, "You don' wanna stop in El Mirage, man. It's more Mexican than here. And you won' get no good recruits in Sun City. They're too old man." I don't know where they ended up, but they never returned to

Surprise again!

I used the same tactic a few months later when another idiot put a sheet on his head and went running through the neighborhood, yelling that he was in the Ku Klux Klan. I sent two black officers to escort him out. They ended up taking him to jail on drug charges. We had better things to deal with than some idiot dressed up like one of the Boo Brothers!

True Love?

When the officer said he was going out with a "suspicious car" that was blocking the entrance to an alley, I didn't think too much about it. I duly noted the time and location and ran the license plate, which came back valid and was registered to an address that was only two or three houses away. I was about to relay that information when the officer said, "They vehicle is rocking. I'm going to look inside."

Things changed very quickly then. He reported that there woman's clothing was strewn all around the outside and believing he may have come upon a rape in progress, requested another unit. When he rapped on the hood of the car, a head appeared over the steering wheel. The engine came to life and the officer believed he was about to get run down.

Then the car started moving in reverse. The officer screamed into the radio, "They saw me! I am in foot pursuit! The vehicle is moving backwards down the alley!"

(Foot pursuit of a vehicle in reverse down an alley? Now *that* must have been a sight!) I didn't even have to call for other units. They were already on the way.

The car pulled backwards into a driveway that matched the address. A woman and man got out of the car, struggling to put their clothes back on. The vehicle was registered to the woman, who had a driver's license to prove she lived at that address. The man was her boyfriend, who also produced a valid operator's license. They explained to the officer that the just wanted to have a little fun.

Not appreciating the adrenaline rush they gave him, the officer yelled, "Well for crying out loud, if it's sex you want, why didn't you just go into the house?"

"We *can't* go in *there!*" the man said.

"Why not?" yelled my officer.

"Because," said the woman, "my *husband* is in there!"

The Killer Bee!

The car had been abandoned in the river bottom for several days. We all knew about it. It wasn't on any private property, it wasn't stolen and no registration existed for it. It just appeared one day, but we never knew when or how. The vehicle was duly tagged for removal and was going to be towed in a day or two. The officers still kept an eye on it when they had time, just to make sure no transients were making a home inside of it.

Naturally, I had to be the one on duty the night one of the cops found it rocking on its rims!

The cop, Ron, was a retired Air Force Captain, who was finishing out a long and distinguished law enforcement career. Short, humorless, a real no nonsense type of guy. I almost felt sorry for the people who were going for a "ride" in a car with no tires on the rims.

The rhythm of the rocking vehicle never broke as the officer approached the car. Obviously, whoever was inside was too engrossed in the action inside the vehicle to pay much attention to the cop who was coming closer and closer. When the officer rapped on the roof with his flashlight, he was a little surprised to see three faces; a male and two females.

The male was a short, skinny little squirt,

maybe one-hundred pounds dripping wet in a wool sweater.

The two women were well over three-hundred pounds each! The little guy explained to the officer that he liked his ladies plump!

All were disheveled and were well passed the legal limit for being drunk. The two women were barely able to stand up. The first one was dressed in all black.

The second woman was dressed in a black skirt and a yellow and black striped blouse. All she needed was a set of feelers on her head and she would look like a three-hundred pound honeybee!

They had broken no laws, and it was obvious that they weren't going to drive the vehicle out of there. But my officer still wanted to FI (field interview) them anyway, for future reference. So he asked them all for identification. The skinny little man and the woman in black readily produced theirs.

The second woman turned around to get her purse out of the car. As she bent over, her short skirt rolled up, revealing the fact that she was not wearing any underwear!

Ron was so startled that his glasses slipped down his nose. He pushed them back and abruptly left the scene, the FI completely forgotten. He no longer cared!

Mr. "No Nonsense" drove directly back to the station and staggered in, holding his hand over his eyes. He was moaning, "I'm blind! I have seen it! I have seen the stinger of the Killer Bee!"

Out On A Limb!

The officer cleared on the radio that he was going out with some people at "the trees," which was just a line of tall trees along a country road in the desert. He spotted an unoccupied vehicle and wanted to make sure it wasn't stolen and dumped there. As he walked around the car, he noticed a lot of clothing strewn haphazardly all over the area. He radioed for another unit, fearing he may have come upon a rape in progress, or even a possible murder scene and a body nearby. There wasn't really any place to hide. The trees along the roadside weren't the best to hide behind and most of the ground was flat, with no ditches or ravines nearby.

The sound of heavy breathing and panting caught the officer's attention so he looked up. Then he spotted them. There were two people on one of the higher branches, making love, high up in the tree somehow balancing on a branch. Making his presence known by shining his flashlight on the two very surprised individuals, he ordered both of the naked people down to the ground. There was obviously no need to search them – indeed, he didn't even want to *touch* them!

He took their names and dates of birth for a

records check. Satisfied that they were both adults and that everything was consensual, he wished them a good time and left the scene, giving them back their privacy. He wondered why anyone would want to climb a tall tree to make out on one of the branches!

He asked me to run a records check on both of the subjects. It turned out the man had a warrant for his arrest, for Non-payment of child support. The officer told me he had already left the scene. I started to shrug it off, but then asked him if he wanted me to go ahead and confirm the warrant.

"Yes, go ahead," he said cheerfully. "I know right where they are!" He requested back up units meet him at the trees. Three other units responded and they went in dark, meaning they turned their headlights off and parked a short distance away.

Sure enough, the couple had climbed back into the tree, though, fortunately for the officers, not quite as high as before. They were completely oblivious to the four approaching policemen.

The man's leg was hanging down as he and the girl tried to balance themselves on the branch. Without hesitation this time, the officer reached up, grabbed his leg and pulled him down.

"Hey, what's the big deal?" the startled

year old man yelled when he recognized the officer from their first meeting. "She's eighteen! She's eighteen!"

"Doesn't matter," said the officer. "Kiss her good bye my man. You're going to jail!"

All the way to the jail, the officers serenaded the man by singing "George George George of the Jungle, look out for that tree!"

Did you say an alligator?

The southwestern deserts of Arizona have a wide variety of wildlife. Often beautiful but deadly. There are coyotes, rattlesnakes, roadrunners, tarantulas and all sorts of other reptiles. But I must admit, I wasn't prepared for the call I received one sunny afternoon.

The man on the 911 line was hysterical and crying. "Help me," he sobbed. "There's an *alligator* in my yard!"

I wasn't sure I had heard him right. "An alligator?" I repeated.

"Yes, an alligator," he said frantically. "A great big one! Please hurry!" I assured him that I would send an officer out right away and told him to stay in his home until the police arrived.

Still, I hesitated before kicking out this call. There was no way I was going to get out of this without some explaining. Nick was the officer on duty for that area, and he always asked for more details! Finally I took a deep breath and cleared him on the radio for traffic. I said, "The gentleman at the address advises that there is an alligator in his yard. Check welfare and advise whether to send out Animal Control or the Phoenix Zoo."

There was a full thirty seconds of radio silence. I was damned if I was going to ask him if he copied. I knew he had heard me! I sat back and decided to wait him out! He finally answered and said, "Radio, I'm not sure whether I heard you correctly. Did you say an *alligator*?"

This was starting to get fun! I jumped on the air. "10-4 sir. AL-LEE-GAY-TOR! A great big one, according to the complainant. I also hear he's hungry!"

"I'll remember this," he said menacingly as he responded to the address.

Taking no chances upon arrival, Nick drove around the premises. The complainant lived on a half acre lot that was covered in dry brush and desert weeds. The officer got on radio and said, "I don't know how an alligator could possibly live out here, unless he's been mummified! There's no water anywhere!"

"I don't make 'em up sir," I responded innocently into the radio. "I just dispatch 'em as I get 'em."

"Yeah, whatever," he said.

Still he was cautious, thinking perhaps that *someone*, either out of malice or for some kind of ill-advised prank may possibly have dumped a real alligator on the guy's property. No one else wanted to respond to help Nick go gator-hunting. He was on his own.

Nick got out of the car and used his retractable baton to beat the brush, keeping his shotgun at the ready with his other hand. It must have been a sight to see the officer swing out his baton and jump back ready to start shooting! He did this for about twenty minutes when the distressed homeowner finally gathered his courage and came out of his house to meet him.

"Officer," he said, "did you find the alligator?"

"Sir," said my now very sweaty officer, "I have been beating this brush for the last twenty minutes and I have not seen an alligator."

Rolling his eyes, the homeowner said, "Well of *course* you can't *see* him. He's invisible!"

"Oh, *that* alligator," responded the quick-witted Nick. "Yes, I almost tripped over that one, and I shooed him away for you."

The man went back into his house and called me to thank me for having such brave, conscientious officers. He very happily said he was going to write a letter to the newspaper about what a fine police department we had and their commitment to the community. (He did, too!)

Nick very firmly informed me that if he was ever forced to go on another alligator call, he was going to have himself a new pair of shoes! I told him to make sure and get a purse for me!

Section Two: Prisoners. We aren't living in Mayberry, USA

The Adventure of the Cottage Cheese

It was one of those quiet evenings in the dispatch center. Absolutely nothing was going on. I was actually able to catch up on some of the never ending clerical work that seemed to grow like algae around the office. I had only done the required radio checks on the officers because there had been no radio traffic, no calls for service, no traffic stops.

I was almost finished with the last report when the peace was shattered by the shrill ringing of the 911 line.

"911, what is your emergency?" I answered.

"Help," the man screamed. "She's wrecking my store! She's wrecking my store!"

I could see by the address on the screen that it was a local Mom and Pop type grocery store. Officers often stopped there to use the restroom or buy snacks throughout their shift. There was hardly ever any trouble there.

"Help is on the way, sir," I said. "Try to calm down. Very briefly, tell me what *she* looks like."

"She's *naked*, man," he screamed. "She naked!"

I wasn't sure I had heard him correctly. "She's *naked?*" I repeated.

"Yeah!" he continued to scream. "She came in my store, took off her clothes and started shaking her bootie in front of everyone! I said, 'Hey, you can't do that here,' and she started wrecking my store!" Suddenly he screamed, "I gotta go!" The line went dead.

I immediately kicked out the call to all of the police units. "Emergency traffic at Pop's Grocery and Liquor," I said. "There's a 918 female destroying the store. Description – she's NAKED guys!" Then I sat back and waited for the units to answer. This was going to be good.

"Charlie Two, enroute."

"Sam Twelve, enroute."

"Bravo Nine, enroute."

"Charlie Seven, enroute."

"Charlie Eighteen, enroute."

I was frankly surprised that no one asked me for a more detailed description of the suspect, as they usually did.

The crazy woman was still at the store when the officers arrived on scene. She was throwing jars of pickles in the condiment aisle and breaking them. When she saw the officers, she immediately began throwing the jars at them! After ducking a jar of sweet relish aimed right at his head, one officer tackled her, causing both of them to land in the dairy case, right on top of the tubs of cottage cheese.

They had been *slimed!*

Three other officers jumped into the fray, and after several slippery tries, managed to get her handcuffed. She was still fighting as they put her in a police car and took her to the El Mirage City Jail for booking.

I couldn't resist the temptation to call my buddy Reymundo in El Mirage dispatch. He needed to know anyway. "Got a good one headed your way," I told him. "918-101 who destroyed a liquor store and fought off four officers."

Judging by the way he was swearing, it was obvious that Reymundo wasn't having a good day. "Oh great," he moaned. "Any more good news?"

"As a matter of fact, yes," I told him. "She's naked."

There was a brief moment of silence on the line as Reymundo absorbed this information. I detected a note of hope in his voice as he asked, "Is she worth looking at?"

"I wouldn't know," I said.

Just then the arresting officer arrived at the El Mirage City Jail and asked for another unit to help him get the combative prisoner out of the backseat. Before I could say another word, an officer that was already booking a prisoner at the EMCJ responded and said he would be waiting outside for him.

"I wondered what he was grumbling about," Reymundo remarked. "He was sore about missing the fight and wanted to see the naked 101."

"Whatever, dude," I responded. "I just want to hang on the phone and listen, if you don't mind. Don't they have to go right past you?"

I didn't have to wait for an answer. At that moment the woman was brought into the station and was fighting again. Being covered with all of that slippery cottage cheese gave her an advantage, and the officers were having a terrible time keeping hold of her. They ended up in a pile on the floor, while Reymundo was yelling, "Threesome! Threesome!"

I couldn't help laughing as my mind showed me a picture of Reymundo sitting there in his baseball cap, cheering on the fight. The officers finally got a good grip on the woman and she was dragged screaming down the hallway to the holding cells.

"Oh man," Reymundo complained. "She ain't even worth looking at!"

"Do tell," I begged.

"She's about 5'2" and over 300 pounds!" I laughed at this information when he started groaning again. "Oh sick," he said. "She's got a big ol' hunk of cottage cheese dropping off her butt!"

I couldn't resist temptation. "Oh man," I said, "I *hope* that's only cottage cheese that's dropping off her butt!"

After cutting loose with a few expletives, Reymundo laughed, "You are a very sick person!"

"Aren't we all?" I asked innocently. He hung up the phone. I got the rest of the story later.

They had put the crazy woman in the female holding cell, but that didn't last; she was fighting with everyone in there. They then took her into the booking room and handcuffed her to the wall, but that didn't work, either. She couldn't get loose, so she promptly stood up, and peed on the officer's shoe!

That was more than enough for the on duty sergeant at the El Mirage jail. He said, "She's outta here!" So the officers would have to book her at the Madison Street Jail in downtown Phoenix.

The woman still put up quite a fight, but was finally re-handcuffed and put into the patrol car for the twenty-minute ride to Madison. I wanted two officers to go in one car, but they said no, the one officer would be fine. I knew that would be a mistake.

On the ride downtown, the woman slipped out of her restraints and began kicking at the patrol car windows as the officer approached a busy intersection coming off the freeway. He announced he was going to pull over to re-handcuff her.

"Don't you dare open that door!" I said into the radio. "All we need is for her to go on television and beg for witnesses who saw you attempt to rape her! You will wait for back up units!" I called Glendale PD and asked them to assist before this woman tried to win the Justice Lottery. They sent four units to the location. Once again there was a struggle, but this time, the woman was completely hog-tied and they completed the trip to Madison.

Just to round out the evening, I decided to call a buddy of mine at the Madison Street Jail. I spoke as sweetly into the phone as I could, but upon hearing my voice, he said only, "Now what?"

"Whatever do you mean?" I asked sweetly.

"I mean, *now what?*" he barked.

"My dear, dear friend," I said. "Why do you always assume that I'm calling you with bad news?"

"Because my dear *friend,*" he responded, "that's the only reason you ever *do* call down here!"

Sounding shocked and appalled, and trying my best to sound hurt, I said, "I'm only calling you because my officer is going to need some help with a combative prisoner."

"Okay, okay," he eased up. "What did this guy do?"

"It's a woman," I corrected him. "She wrecked a liquor store. She's 918. She likes to fight with policemen and is very good at slipping out of restraints. Oh by the way," I added gleefully, "she's overweight and naked and *slimed* with cottage cheese! Have a good evening!"

I quickly hung up before he could respond. I'm sure he never forgave me.

A Really Stupid Criminal

There were so many times that I was positive I had seen it all. That I couldn't possibly see anything new, or that I had seen the absolute epitome of stupidity. Then without fail, there would come a situation that proved that I hadn't seen anything yet!

The person on the 911 line was hysterical. "They're running, they're running, they're running, they're running, they're running, they're running!"

"Calm down," I ordered. "*Who's* running? What's going on there?"

"*They* are," the woman screamed. "Down the alley!"

Impatiently, I said, "Ma'am, who are *'they,'* which was is 'down the alley,' and what did *they* do that they are *running* for?"

Hysterically she screamed, *"They stole my pit bull!"*

I dispatched some officers to the address. After all, a burglary is a burglary. While the officers were on scene, taking the report, the dog arrived home, triumphantly carrying a piece of someone's bloody shirt in his big jaws and appearing to be very pleased with his trophy as he dropped at his owner's feet.

The dog had rescued himself!

I went ahead and notified area hospitals to call us if someone came in with a dog bite that they couldn't quite explain. Within the hour, we received a call of a guy with a huge piece of his chest flesh missing – that somehow corresponded with the big rip in his shirt, that just happened to match the bloody piece that "Adolph" had carried home to his owner!

The idiot was charged with burglary. I wish there was a way to charge him with gross stupidity. He would have received life in prison!

Mando

Out of the many notables in the neighborhood, there is always that one notable that stands out as above (or far below) the rest. In this case, it was Mando. He was a complete jerk. A little gang-banger wannabe, that any "decent" gang would have rejected, no matter how low their standards for recruitment. He looked almost as intelligent as he was, with his eyebrows knit into one long, continuous line. His nose had been broken so many times that it was crooked. (I always thought that they should have broken his jaw to teach him to keep his mouth shut!) He was so skinny from snorting cocaine that it was a wonder his skinny carcass was still walking around. His big thing to prove how tough he was would be to bang on the door of a senior citizen and challenge an 80 year old man to come out and fight. We all knew that someday, something serious would happen because of Mando.

I was the lucky girl on duty the day it did. I received a 911call from a passing motorist about a man down, lying in a pool of blood. We had also had a report of a possible shotgun blast in the same area. When officers arrived on the scene, they discovered it was Mando. He was still alive, but was in pretty bad shape. No one was crying very hard, but they shipped him off to the hospital anyway.

It was hours before we learned what had happened. Mr. Big-and-Bad had been walking down the street when a group of angry residents began chasing him. Mando ran like a typical coward. What was amazing that even though literally dozens of people saw him being chased, no one called the police. Instead, they joined the posse and went after him. One of the residents had a shotgun, and was just waiting for the first opportunity to use it.

Unfortunately for Mando, he was wearing loose shorts and no underwear. He was exhausted from running and the people behind him were gaining ground. Mando desperately tried to jump over a chain link fence, and the deafening blast of the shotgun filled the air, which attracted the attention of the passing motorist. (The motorist later gave a statement to the effect that, had he known it was Mando, he would have driven on by.)

Blood was pouring out everywhere, and Mando hit the ground. The crowd dispersed, apparently satisfied and convinced that he had been hit. They went their own way and left him there to die.

But Mando hadn't been shot.

The chain link fence was in *dire* need of repair. When officers returned to the area to inspect the crime scene, the found Mando's testicle, still caught on one of the rusty, loose prongs, baking in the hot July Arizona sun.

Mando would never win any awards for intelligence. His last burglary was the end of him. He decided to break into a home and stole the owner's pet canaries. All fifty of them.

This woman refused to be a victim. She doggedly worked the phones, calling every pet store in the valley, until she found the one that bought fifty canaries from a guy for one-dollar each. The pet store owner refused to do business without some identification, so Mando produced his driver's license – which was suspended – and drove away with the cash. He was caught and sentenced to prison, where he was duly christened with the name "Bird Man of Florence."

KatieAnn

Another of our "notables" was KatieAnn-*that's-one-word*-Stephens. Now, I rarely met any of the prisoners under desirable circumstances, but she really took the prize for obnoxious.

The Sheriff's Office had arrested her on an outstanding warrant. She was in her mid-50s but she was strong. She had really given the deputies a bad time when they brought her into the station so that she could be searched by a female cop or dispatcher. There were no female officers on duty anywhere close, nor any other female dispatchers. When they called our police agency, the Chief said that I would be in there in a few minutes and would be "delighted" to search their combative female prisoner. (I knew I should have called in sick that day!)

This broad had been around and wasn't going to give in easy. Even though I was surrounded by deputies and our own officers, I knew that this could go bad really fast. Another fight and another charge wouldn't matter to her at all.

She screamed at me, "You come near me girlie, and I will kick your ass!"

Then again, I hadn't had a good fight in a long time.

"Listen, toots," I said, deliberately keeping my voice low and trying to sound bored, "we can do this the easy way, with you cooperating, or the hard way, with me putting you in the hospital in intensive care. Doesn't matter much to me. I get paid either way. Now what is it going to be?"

She seemed to be sizing me up as well. Without taking my eyes off of her, I told the cops, "If she comes at me, keep your asses out of this. She's mine."

KatieAnn apparently decided that it wasn't worth the risk. She turned around and put her hands on the wall. She couldn't help taking one more shot at me and sneered, "Just don't enjoy it too much, you lesbian whore!"

Still keeping my voice deliberately low, I said to her, "KatieAnn, I like my women a lot younger and a lot skinnier, and you ain't got a damn thing I want. I don't like blonds at any age or size, so you don't have a thing to worry about."

She freaked out and began screaming for the cops to get me away from her. I slammed her into the wall and asked her if she really wanted to have a go. Deciding to play into her homophobia, I told her, "Come on KatieAnn. You know you like it rough." One of the deputies laughed so hard, he peed his pants. She was soon on her way.

After she left, the Chief looked at me, grinning and said, "Now, I *know* you're not gay!"

Shrugging my shoulders, I said, "No, I'm not, but *she* didn't know that."

Soon after that, KatieAnn moved from the Sheriff's jurisdiction and into ours! She became a regular caller, a regular Pain-In-My-Ass. The last time I saw her, she was arrested for using a rock to smash out the window of a car right in front of my police officer. When booking her, I asked her for her name. She said, "KatieAnn, that's one word, Stephens! Get it right! It isn't Katie Ann. It's KatieAnn."

I shrugged, and said, "Got it. First name KatieAnn. Last name Stephens. Middle name THAT'S ONE WORD." I entered that on the booking sheet and the next time we put out on a warrant for her, I added it to her alias names.

I couldn't believe this obnoxious person used to be a nurse's aid at a nursing home! Then again, I thought I understood exactly why she wasn't any longer.

Delores

Delores was a former legal secretary. "Former" being the keyword. The woman was completely nuts. I used to take a secret delight in sending the rookie cops to her residence when she called, to welcome them into the unreal world of police work at its finest! (NOT)

I made it a point to never advise them that she was a major "918"! (918 is the police code for INSANE PERSON.)

Delores once called 911, screaming, "My house is on fire!" Fire and police units were dispatched, only to find her standing on the sidewalk, holding on to her purse with a pouty look on her face. She said there was no real fire. She just wanted the cops to get there faster.

She was cited.

According to Delores, burglaries occurred at her home at least once a week. She reported that someone had stolen her jacuzzi, used it and brought it back. Another time she reported that her car had been stolen, driven exactly 3.2 miles and returned to the driveway. Another time, she had smeared bright red fingernail polish on her doorknobs, and insisted that she had caught the burglars fingerprints on the doors.

Another night, she called to report that

someone had broken into her house and left a big mess in her bathroom, with "brown stuff all over the place in there!" I was groaning inwardly as I dispatched the call, figuring the officers would never forgive me.

It wasn't what I thought. There was brown hair dye all over the bathroom, which mysteriously matched the new brown color of her hair.

Her major problem was with the neighbors. She reported that her Mexican next-door neighbors (*Those damn Mexicans again!*) were using their electric skillet to manipulate their ESP vibrations to go next door to harass her. These same Mexicans were in direct communication with the UFO that regularly buzzed the town and landed on her roof. These space aliens had planted a bunch of little people to live under her carpet. In a fit one day, she tore up all of her carpeting, and we all breathed a sigh of relief, figuring this may end the problem.

No such luck. The little people just moved into her attic where they had barbecues, and stole her encyclopedias and her panties. When the fire trucks arrived that night, she told the fire captain that they were having a barbecue right then, and she wanted him to go up there and turn the fire hose on them. The Captain declined, but did offer to turn the fire hose on her for making a phony call.

She called the station very aggravated one night, because the Mexicans were using their ESP again. Then she haughtily asked me, "You *do* know what ESP is, don't you?"

Faking my best Massachusetts accent, I said, "Lady, I come from Salem. *Of course* I know what ESP is!" She hung up on me, not for the first time, but sadly, not for the last.

I was very good at faking accents. It got to the point that Delores loved me on the phone, but hated me in person. She never knew I was the same person. Whenever she called, I would put her through to "Sgt. Murphy" (*Moiphy*) and deal with her that way.

I couldn't get rid of her so easily when she decided to come into the station. She came storming in, very agitated, early one Sunday morning, demanding to see the Chief of Police. Trying to sound as bored as possible, I said, "He's not here, Delores."

"Where is he?" she screamed.

"Probably sleeping," I shrugged. "It's 6 AM on a Sunday morning, Delores. How many Chief's of Police do you know that are at the station at 6 AM on a Sunday morning?"

Undeterred, she demanded, "Then I want to speak to the Captain!"

Rolling my eyes, I said, "We're a *small*

agency, Delores. We *don't have* a Captain."

"Then I want to see the Lieutenant!"

Knocking on my head, I said, "Delores? **Small agency.** We don't have a Lieutenant, either."

Raising her voice, she said, "I want the Sergeant, then!"

"*Sunday morning!* He takes the day off!"

She was literally stamping her foot and yelling by this point. "Then I want to speak to the highest ranking officer that is here!"

Well, that was the rookie, Carlos. He was a handsome young Mexican American man, who didn't look Hispanic, had been kicked loose just a few days before. Glancing over towards the patrol room, I saw him in the doorway, frantically waving his hands at me and mouthing *NO!*

Fighting back a grin, I said, "I will call him in right now for you, ma'am." I got on the radio and cleared his number, "Lincoln-9. Come in to meet the citizen at the 103 (station)."

Carlos *had* to answer me on the radio, so he said, "I just got to the 103, ma'am. I'll be there in a minute." It was amazing how he could sound so *professional* on the radio while flipping me the bird from the patrol room! I was actually impressed by his multi-tasking!

I could tell he was struggling to keep a

straight face as he went into the lobby and introduced himself to her. He was able to maintain the straight face when Delores demanded, "I want you to make the FBI *stop* watching my house!"

Wishing I had some popcorn, I sat back in my chair to watch him struggle for a while with her. He committed the cardinal sin among policemen: He tried to reason with a lunatic.

"Delores," he said reasonably, "the FBI *is not* watching your house. They would notify the local agency that they were in the area, watching a suspect for this reason or that so that in case there were any calls about suspicious subjects in the area, the local agency would be able to deal with the situation without endangering the FBI agents or their own officers." (Would they? I really want to know!)

Their exchange lasted for several minutes. Finally, I got bored and decided to rescue Carlos. I said, "Carlos, come in here and watch radio. Let me talk with Delores." He made his escape gladly.

Stepping into the lobby, I tried to speak in as bored a tone as possible. "Delores, the FBI is definitely *not* watching your house."

"How would *you* know?" she sneered.

"Because," I retorted with all the authority I could muster, "the ***CIA watches*** the FBI. They know *everything* that the FBI does. Believe me, Delores, the CIA would *know* if the FBI was watching your house."

She appeared to be confused now. "How do you know?

Faking my best Russian accent, I said, "Because I vatch zee CIA. I know *everytink dat* goes on around here, *dahlink*."

She then backed away from me, screaming something about me being an undercover commie something-or-other. I wasn't really listening to her, but I knew it wasn't very nice. She turned on her heel and marched out in a huff.

Not wanting to leave things in such a negative place, I hurried after her, and called out in my best Spanish accent, *"Adios amiguita!"* Really, it was early on a Sunday morning. Can I truly be blamed for *forgetting* how much she hated Spanish?

Delores and I finally came to a "truce" of sorts a couple of year later. After I had my son, she came into the station for one of her many reports – which strangely, she hadn't done throughout my entire pregnancy. She was surprised to learn that I had a child now. I showed her a picture of my baby, which she "ooh'd" and "aah'd" over – and then I realized that this was a lonely individual. Her calls for "service" became much less frequent and she would call instead to ask how my baby was doing.

The Nurse

The shift had barely started and I had just settled in my chair in the radio room, when a man with blood dripping from his face walked into the lobby. He wanted to speak to a police officer right away, and he needed paramedics. Someone had obviously dug all five claws into the right side of his face, and his clothes were saturated.

"What happened?" I asked.

"My drunk girlfriend attacked me in the car and clawed my face while I was driving her to work!"

Before I could say or do anything else, the girlfriend was on him like a tigress, clawing him on the left side of his face. The fight was on, literally two feet away from me. Without hesitation, I got on the radio and shouted, "Fight at the 103, domestic violence in progress at the 103 lobby. Get in here guys and save your dispatcher!" I grabbed the phone and called the Chief in his office on the intercom.

"I can't understand you," he said. "There's too much noise."

"Chief!" I shouted! "We have a domestic violence in progress in the lobby! Grab your gun and get out here!"

"I can't hear you," he said again.

The fight moved out into the parking lot. I jumped on the radio as I was shouting at the Chief on the phone. "The fight is in the parking lot. The fight is in the parking lot outside the front door!"

"I can't understand you," he said again. He hung up and came down the hallway just as two units pulled up outside and separated the combatants. "Now what's going on?" he demanded.

Waving my hand dismissively at him, completely irritated and with my pulse racing, I said sarcastically, "Go back to sleep Chief. There was a domestic violence in the lobby which moved outside, but the guys are here now."

"I wondered what all the noise was," he said as he hurried out the door. He mentioned all of the blood that was in the lobby. I grabbed a camera and took pictures as they handcuffed the woman outside and prepared to bring her in. She was still very agitated and violent as they brought her into the patrol room.

It was then that I saw her in a nurse's uniform!

The badly injured man also came in. I called paramedics for him, and then was given the dubious honor of having to search the woman. They thought all of the fight had left her, so they removed her handcuffs so that I could search her. She turned on me suddenly, trying to claw me, so I laid her out and threw her butt to the floor before she knew what happened.

"Listen, you drunken bitch," I sneered, pressing my knee into her neck as I pushed her head hard into the floor. "I have one nerve left and you just got on it. I've got to search you and you're going to take it and like it. If I have to put your ass down again, it's going to take six paramedics to scrape up what's left of you! Now do we understand each other?" She was screaming, calling me a bitch. I twisted her arm tightly behind her back, and said, "You know what I do when people call me a *bitch,* honey? I *prove* it!" She finally came to the realization that I wasn't like her boyfriend, and that I didn't care about hurting her, so she became much more cooperative. To prove my point, I yanked her off the floor and slammed her into the wall while I conducted the search. I then half carried her into the cell and helped her to the bunk and told her to stay there until the door closed, or I could *make* her stay there until an ambulance came. After I slammed the door, the Chief stared at me in amazement. "I didn't know you had that in you, Beth," he said. He was grinning.

One of the officers quipped, "That's because you don't usually work the swing shift, boss!"

The fight started because she was very drunk and insisting on going to work at the hospital. Her boyfriend didn't want her going in drunk, and said that she was going to get fired. She attacked him in the car at that point, which was just around the corner from the police station. He drove in and the rest was history. He was more than willing to press charges. He said he would be packed and gone from the house before she got out of jail – after he got out of the hospital.

At the mention of the hospital, the nurse was howling that she had to call in so her supervisor would know that she couldn't make it in. I promptly dialed the number to the hospital, put it on speakerphone and asked for her supervisor. When she came on the line, I introduced myself. "Nurse Jones won't be in tonight," I said, "because she assaulted her boyfriend and two police officers while drunk. By the way, she was on her way to work and in uniform when this happened. We're going to make her take a breathalyzer later, and we'll call you with the results, if you want to know them. Just so you'll be aware of the level of patient care she would have provided tonight." (She later blew a .14 BAC)

The supervisor said that Nurse Jones didn't need to bother coming back to work at all. She would be fired.

Hanging up the phone, I told Nurse Jones, "Now you don't need to be worried about being late to work. Now you don't have a job."

A few minutes later, the Chief was going through the contents of her purse in order to inventory everything that was in there. She began screaming at him that he had "better not steal the $800 cash she had in there!" He was showing more patience than I was, but as it was him doing the inventory of her purse, I wasn't about to open my mouth. He said, "I'm laying everything out right here so you can see it. I will count your money right in front of you, so you can see exactly where it will go."

"Well," she said, "if you'll just let me go, you can *keep* the $800."

Looking up at her, he said, "I'm sorry, I didn't hear you."

"I said you can keep the money if you'll just open the door and let me go."

Turning to me, he said, "Did you hear that?"

"Yes, sir," I said, knowing I would have to now be a witness to an attempted bribery. As he counted out her money, I couldn't help remarking, "Boy, what an idiot! If you're going to attempt to bribe someone, you should at least have the right amount of cash on you!" She only had $7 in her purse – and most of that in loose change.

They finally had everything ready for the ride to jail. I stood right there while they opened the door. Glancing at me, she asked the officer, "She isn't coming, is she?"

"Only her golden voice over the radio," he said cheerfully.

Carrying my portable radio, I grabbed the Chief's arm and led him to the still bloody lobby. I waved my arm around the room and said simply, "I'm not cleaning this up!"

He called in a service that he had contracted but never had the opportunity to use. They usually cleaned up bloody crime scenes after a dead body had been removed. It was the first time they had to clean up so much blood from a police station.

Section Three: OMG These People Are Multiplying!

A New Low In Stupidity

The 21-year old woman on the 911 phone line was strangely calm, considering that she was standing barefoot in the gravel at a gas station pay phone.

She was crying on the phone as she told me she had been having very bad pains in her stomach all day and it was getting worse. My mind was racing with the possibilities of food poisoning, drug or alcohol or appendicitis. One by one she denied everything.

I dispatched fire and EMS units to the scene, but they were a long way off, not having yet returned from another call in the boonies. El Mirage Fire Department was also tied up on another call and couldn't respond. I dispatched officers to the scene and tried to keep her calm until help could arrive on scene. "I tried to walk to my sister's house," she sobbed, "but the pain just got too bad so I decided to call you."

"Well," I said soothingly, "the paramedics are on the way and we'll get you to a hospital and try to find out what's wrong with you."

She suddenly started moaning and crying badly as the pain intensified. "Oh my God," she screamed. "I hope this doesn't hurt the baby!"

I felt like I had been slapped in the face. "*What* baby?" I asked.

"I'm pregnant," she said, and began yelling again.

A light went on in my head as I realized that the pains had been coming at regular intervals. I silently kicked myself for not making the connection. But then again, wouldn't a pregnant woman know enough to *tell* me she was pregnant?

"How far along are you?" I asked, trying to keep my voice level and keep the irritation out.

"The baby is two weeks late," she responded.

"Is this your first child?"

"No," she said. "It's my fourth." She was 21 and fourth kid? Yet she couldn't tell she was in labor?

"Your fourth?" I said incredulously. "*How* old are you again?"

"I'm twenty-one," she said. "Do you think the baby is coming?"

"Yes, ma'am, I certainly do think that the baby is coming."

She told me she wanted to hang up and would try to make it to her sister's house. Naturally, she didn't know the address.

"Don't you dare even think about leaving there," I said firmly. "You stay put so we can find you. I will have you arrested if you try to leave!" She believed me.

Then she let out another long moan. I asked her if she was sitting down.

"I'm standing up," she wailed.

I could just imagine the baby falling out and landing head first on that hard gravel. "Sit down you fool!" I yelled.

Finally my officer arrived on scene and said she was sitting on the ground screaming. (I already knew that!) "10-4," I responded, then cleared the EMS. "Engine One, be advised this 101 is 9 ½ months pregnant and is in labor."

"Her first?" asked the fire captain.

"Negative," I responded. "Her fourth!"

"We're on scene," they said.

The officer immediately left, not wanting to be around to witness a birth.

Two minutes later, the fire captain got back on the air, asking for the ETA (Estimated Time of Arrival) for the ambulance.

It was a boy.

Section Four: I Should Have Stayed Home!

UFO's

The Goodyear Blimp was in the sky and the local nuts were on the telephone, absolutely convinced that we were being invaded from outer space and the War of the Worlds was about to start.

One woman kept calling back, completely undeterred by the fact that I kept hanging up on her. She was screaming that *they* were shooting their laser lights into her house and she needed to know what to do. I wasn't about to send officers to this nutcase. They would have made me miserable!

She was a piece of cake compared to the man who kept calling me. He wasn't about to be soothed with any of my sage advice. He wanted officers to fight off the invasion!

Finally I said, "Sir we can't do a thing about those UFOs until they land and start speeding down 111th Avenue! We are only *street* cops," I explained. "What you need are the *sky* cops! You need to report this to the Air Force!" I didn't give him a number, figuring he would never be able to find it.

Twenty-minutes later, I was still congratulating myself on my cleverness when the non-emergency line rang and a sergeant from Luke Air Force Base was on the other end.

"Are you the *nut* who told that *other* nut to call us about that damned blimp?" he asked sternly.

"Yes, sir, that is me," I said as sweetly as possible. "Aren't you the 'sky cops' who patrol the wild blue yonder?"

He was chuckling as he answered, "Girlfriend, we are going to find out where you live!"

Completely un-intimidated, I asked, "So how did you handle him?"

"We've hung up on him three times," said the sergeant. "He keeps calling back."

Together we concocted a story to pass on to the guy. We would tell him that Mars was at war with Mercury. The Martians made a treaty with the President of the United States to take the nuclear waste from the Palo Verde Nuclear Power Plant as fuel, which would clean up our environment, and take the war to Mercury. "From the mind of one lunatic to another," he mused. "I'll try it."

The man called back while I was on with the Sergeant, so he placed me on hold while he gave the guy our story. He swore him to a secret and sacred oath, calling upon his patriotism as an American, and let him in on a "National Secret" that could never be revealed to the American public. The guy swallowed the story whole. The sergeant decided to give me a "stay" of execution and we hung up.

Once again, I was congratulating myself on my cleverness when the guy called me back. He promptly told me everything he had vowed to keep secret. He said, "You know I would much rather that Mars win the war than Mercury."

"Me too," I said. "Obviously the President does too. But these calls have to stop, sir. They are all being recorded." He finally seemed to understand and hung up.

I called the sergeant back. "He told me everything," I said. "Can we kill him now?"

The man called back to verify the White House address was 1600 Pennsylvania Ave in Washington, DC. He was going to write a letter to President Roosevelt to congratulate him for doing such a fine job. He didn't specify whether he meant Franklin or Teddy. I wasn't about to ask him, either.

Besides, I just didn't have the heart to tell him that the President was now George H. W. Bush.

The Martian Attack

The woman on the phone was absolutely livid. The "martians" were attacking and we weren't doing anything about it. "They" were shooting laser lights into her windows and she was demanding police protection!

At first, I thought she had to be joking. Then I realized we had a brand new nutcase living in the neighborhood. Fortunately, she had not called 911 so I wasn't obligated to send an officer to her residence. The guys would have not been pleased to deal with this – they had been running crazy all night long with other real calls. Still I asked for her address.

"Ma'am," I said, "I can't send an officer to your house right now."

"What am I supposed to do?" she screamed.

"Put aluminum foil over all of your windows," I told her.

"Aluminum foil?" She seemed confused.

That was a good sign for me. "Yes, ma'am," I said. "That will reflect their lasers right back at them and they will destroy themselves!As you can imagine, the officers are all busy battling with the military, trying to beat back these martians." I also advised her to get under her kitchen table and stay there until the battle was won. I repeated, "The foil will turn their death rays right back at them and they'll end up destroying themselves. That will be the best thing you can do to help out."

She thanked me profusely and hung up. At that same moment, one of the officers checked out at the station for his lunch break.

Her address was just around the corner. I said, "Let me heat up your food for you. I want you to take a drive around the corner." I explained what was going on, so he agreed to drive past her house.

He returned to the station shaking his head. "Is she really putting up the foil?" I asked.

"You should have seen those curtains shaking as she was putting up foil!" he said. "She had already completely covered up two of her windows and the big window in the living room was half covered and the draperies were moving all over the place. I don't think she even saw me."

We groaned at the thought of having to deal with her in the future. But the foil apparently worked. We never had a call to her house again. I wonder whether or not she ever came out from under that kitchen table!

Section Five: On The Road Again!

The Pursuit

I will never forget my first experience dealing with a high speed pursuit. Mainly because at the time it happened, I had never been trained how to handle one! That wasn't covered during the six-week training period. And I had been on the job all of six months.

The evening started out quietly, as most troublesome shifts did. A few traffic stops, a few warnings. No radio calls to speak of. I was beginning to think that weeknight shifts were very boring.

Then the officer cleared on the radio. "I'm southeast on Grand, behind a yellow Buick four door that is failing to yield to my lights."

My stomach began to tighten up in knots. I didn't realize then that it was one of the *symptoms* of an impending pursuit. The officer was also brand new – he started working at the department the same day I did. His voice was showing the strain as he said, "The vehicle is still not yielding."

I got on the phone and called Peoria PD, telling them that my officer was headed in their direction. "I've tried the siren," the officer reported, "and the vehicle is still not yielding. He's picking up speed." The Peoria PD dispatcher had barely picked up the phone, listening to my report of the situation headed in their direction, when she heard my officer over the phone, "I'm in pursuit, southeast on Grand, 75 mph, yellow Buick four door. Fully loaded." (Fully loaded meant there were numerous passengers.)

The vehicle was doing 100 mph by the time it reached the Peoria City Limits. My officer was still behind it when our Sergeant broke in and ordered, "Discontinue the pursuit."

Not about to give up on the situation, a Peoria PD Sergeant on duty took up the pursuit where my officer left off. As he said later, "I was the only sergeant on duty and I give myself permission." My officer followed behind the Peoria sergeant, not "in pursuit," but to provide backup. His role at this time was completely as support.

The suspect vehicle continued southeast on Grand Avenue, going through the cities of Peoria, Glendale and finally Phoenix, reaching speeds of over 110 mph and causing three injury accidents. The vehicle finally reached the six-way intersection of Thomas, Grand and 27th Avenue, where the driver lost control and crashed into the back of a brand new Chevy Blazer. Fortunately, the Chevy had airbags, so the driver wasn't seriously hurt. The suspect driver and one of his passengers jumped out of the car and started running. One of the occupants, a juvenile offender, was injured in the vehicle. He gave up without a fight. The second juvenile offender was tackled by Phoenix PD as he tried to run from the scene with his banged up knees.

The third suspect, an adult male, managed to break into the car dealership that was on the northeast corner of the intersection. Rather than risk officers going in after him, they waited for the K-9 unit to arrive. The Phoenix cops yelled into the building, ordering the suspect to come out or they would send in the dog.

He didn't.

They did!

After numerous barks, growls, bites and high-pitched, hysterical, girlish screams later, the suspect emerged from the car dealership, with all of the fight totally gone from him. The owner of the Chevy Blazer was still being treated for his injuries by Phoenix firefighter paramedics. He was absolutely sick over the loss of his beloved Blazer, which he had just purchased that day, brand new off the lot. When he saw the suspect being led out in handcuffs, his eyes grew wide with angry recognition, and the man exploded. The Chevy owner was an off-duty parole officer with a badge. He *recognized* his parolee, now wearing the pretty silver bracelets and covered in dog bites and blood.

The yellow Buick turned out to be stolen, though the theft had not been discovered by the owner. The juveniles were also on parole, having barely been released from the Adobe Mountain Juvenile facility the week before. There were over $100,000 worth of diamonds that had been stolen during a burglary from a jewelry store in Sun City West, which was at that moment being investigated by the fine deputies of the Maricopa County Sheriff's Office, completely unaware that the crime was already solved and the suspect was in painful custody.

Nor did the Parole Officer know any of that yet. He wouldn't have cared if he did. Throwing down the bloody ice pack given to him by the paramedics for his own open head wound, he lunged at his parolee, scoring a well-aimed punch to the guy's face, and had to be grabbed and held back by three police officers. The parolee was cowering, knowing he was done.

"You lying son of a bitch!" the Parole Officer screamed. *"You told me you had a job!"*

"He *did*," quipped my officer, Jim, who absolutely was *not* helping the situation. "This was *it!*"

When he returned to the station, Jim told me that he hadn't even planned on running the license plate. He just wanted to ask the driver to slow down a little while driving through the construction zone. But he learned his lesson. From that day on, he always ran every person, every license plate, every time. Jim turned out to be one of the finest cops I ever knew.

Needless to say, the suspect's parole was revoked, and he went back to prison. It just BUH-ROKE my heart.

By The Grace Of God And The Dispatcher

The officer, Ron Jackson, sounded absolutely cheerful as he announced yet another traffic stop on Grand Avenue. "Get ready for another ticket!" He was thoroughly enjoying himself that night.

I threw down my pen in frustration, because I was trying to get through that large stack of reports. This guy had been a ticket-writing machine tonight! I would never get through the stack at this rate. Dutifully, I noted the location and ran the license plate he gave me.

I got the shock of my life. The license plate came back to the pastor of my church!

Pastor and his wife had gone to Prescott for the day. They didn't realize that Pastor had forgotten his wallet, until they were nearly there. Fortunately, his wife had cash and credit cards and had paid for everything while they were there, and they had a perfectly lovely day in every way. They started back late in the day, so it was dark when they arrived back in the valley.

There is a certain point on Grand Avenue where the speed limit drops suddenly. Because Pastor and his wife were talking, and because it was dark, he didn't see the one warning sign, so he was caught by my officer. They realized what had happened when they saw Jackson's flashing lights in their rear view mirror.

"Oh no," said the Pastor's wife.

My officer approached them, tall and intimidating. Ever the true professional, he asked the Pastor for his driver's license, registration and proof of insurance.

Pastor was mortified. He explained about the forgotten wallet, which had his license, and his brand new proof of insurance card that he had put in there when it arrived in the mail the previous day. He said, "I'm a minister, Officer, and I am so embarrassed. I never, ever speed, or break any of the laws. I'm just beside myself."

Ron Jackson was completely unsympathetic. He merely cited the laws that Pastor had broken, told them he was going to cite him for each one, and answered the Pastor's questions about how much each violation could possibly cost him. Pastor and his wife were very upset over the amount of money that could possibly be involved. My officer absolutely did not believe that this man was a minister. One thing he had always said was that "people lie to the police." He had heard the "minister" line before.

I was frantically trying to call Ron on his cellular phone, but it was turned off. When the officer cleared on radio, giving the Pastor's name and date of birth, I took the information, automatically running it. As I knew it would be, his "record" was clean. I got on the radio, and said, "Call me. NOW!"

"Can it wait?" he asked.

"Negative! Call me NOW!"

When he called, I cut loose. "Don't you dare give that man a ticket! He's the pastor of my church!"

Dumbfounded, Officer Jackson said, "He's *your* pastor?" He gave a short laugh, and added, "I thought that minister stuff was just a line!"

"Well, it's *not* a line and he's my pastor! And if he was speeding, there was a darned good reason!"

"Calm down, Beth," he said.

"No I won't calm down! Don't you dare give him a ticket!" Grasping at straws, I said, "You're Catholic, aren't you?"

"Yes," he said carefully.

"What would happen if you gave a ticket to a priest?"

He quipped, "I would probably go to hell."

"Well, buster," I seethed, "Hell's fires are ten times hotter for the poor cop who gives a ticket to the Pentecostal Preacher! He's a holy roller! You leave him alone!"

He was laughing as he hung up on me. I knew everything would be all right.

Pastor and his wife, however, had been sweating the entire time in their car, dreading the ticket that they were sure was coming. When my officer emerged from his police car, his wife said, "Oh dear, here it comes." They were both groaning and ready to cry.

Officer Jackson poked his head through their window, handed back their registration and said pleasantly, "Let's slow it down a little, Preacher. Have a good evening." He was halfway back to his patrol car and was so startled that he jumped by a very loud "PRAISE THE LORD!" coming from the Pastor's car.

I couldn't wait to corner Pastor at church the following evening. I strolled up to him casually, greeted him and asked him how his trip to Prescott was. He asked how I knew about it.

"Because," I said, "my officer told me all about it."

The look on his face was priceless. Then he said, "*Your* officer?"

Smiling, I said, "Yup! I'm the reason he *didn't* give you a ticket!"

"Praise Jesus!" Pastor yelled. He got in front of the entire congregation that night, to my surprise, and "confessed" the entire episode. He said that his experience was proof that God was surely watching out for His own, because He had placed me behind the radio that night to protect the Pastor.

I was only interested in whether or not the officer had been polite to the pastor or if he had been in a "stinker" mood. Pastor assured me the officer had been stern but kind.

I called Ron when we were both on duty the following Monday Night. "You're off the hook," I said. I related to him what Pastor had said.

"Well," remarked my officer sourly, "God sure *does* work in mysterious ways!"

"What do you mean by that?" I asked.

"You can tell your Pastor that God was looking out for him by sending the devil *herself* to protect him!" he snapped and hung up the phone.

Now that remark could not go unanswered! This was *war!*

Hannah

Hannah was another one of the more "colorful" residents of Surprise. Translation: she was NUTS! She had a "special gift" in that she could see things that no one else could.

It didn't matter that the things she saw weren't really there. She called 911 anyway to report them. Her most often reported incidents involved the invisible naked people who would go streaking through the streets of her neighborhood. She was always afraid that someone would be offended by their invisible naked bodies.

"Hannah," I would ask, messing with her, "if they're *invisible,* how could anyone possibly be *offended?"*

She would haughtily retort that there were other gifted people like herself who could see through their invisibility. It didn't matter that she wasn't offended. She was worried about "the others." I had long before given up telling her there were no others like her.

I was never sure whether it was these same invisible naked people or different ones that would come in and sit naked on top of her refrigerator. How could I tell? They were invisible, after all! Officer Jackson *especially* hated being sent to check out the 911 calls from this escapee from La La Land. I always tried to space out the calls between the officers, so that they wouldn't have a steady diet of ANY nutcase. But tonight, I was on a mission!

Officer Jackson had just called me "the devil herself." He had challenged me! I couldn't let it go unanswered.

I hadn't had any calls for service from Hannah for several days. Rather than waiting to let nature take its normal course, I decided to call her from the unrecorded line.

"Hello, Hannah," I said sweetly. "This is Beth from the Surprise Police Department.

She sounded surprised. "What's wrong?"

(Now that was a switch in dialogue!) "I was just concerned about you," I said, "because I haven't heard from you for a few days, and I just wanted to make sure that you were all right."

"Well," she said simply, "I just decided to stop calling."

Groaning inwardly at my lost opportunity for peace, I asked, "Why is that, Hannah?"

"Well," she said again, "I just didn't feel like anyone cared."

"Of course I care, Hannah," I lied. "Is everything all right?"

"No," she said. "Not really."

"What's going on?"

"The usual stuff that no one ever believes

me about."

"Are those people bothering you again?" I prodded her.

"Yes, they are!" I could tell she was getting steamed.

"Would you like to speak to Officer Jackson?"

"Yes I would!"

"I will send him right out," I said. After all, it was a very dull, quiet night. We had to do something to liven up things.

Needless to say, Ron wasn't too thrilled with the idea of going out to see Hannah. He called me and asked why I was sending him, because it wasn't his turn. I said, "Because that's what the DEVIL HERSELF does, Ron."

He was silent for a moment. Then, "Are you really mad about that?"

"Are you speaking to *moi?*" I asked innocently. Then, "It's a call for service, Ron. Plain and simple. And if Hannah gets herself a pet cop in the process, well, consider that to be part of protecting and serving the public." This time, I hung up on him. Ron was her pet for the next several shifts.

Finally, he had enough and called me again. Ron was very sweet for several minutes, before finally asking, "Are you mad because I called you the Devil?"

"What? Me? Mad? Whatever gave you THAT idea?"

He gave a big sigh on the other end of the phone. "I apologize. I didn't mean it."

"Yes, you did," I corrected him. "I'm mad because you hung up on me."

He apologized profusely, promising to never hang up on me again. After that, whenever Hannah called, I rotated the calls between the cops. Ron was glad. But the rest of the guys were furious. They had enjoyed their little "vacation" from her. But I always had the threat of giving her another "pet" to keep them in line!

But Seriously Folks...

There is no way to prepare for every single type of emergency that may arise, but I can say with authority that not all of them require a call to 911. A busted water pipe requires a *plumber*, not a police officer. We can all do simple thing to help us help the rescuers, if and when that situation arises.

1. Keep a list of addresses for your friends and relatives, and keep the list updated as necessary. The 911 operator can't help you if you know that there is an emergency, but you can't tell them where it is.
2. For out of state friends and relatives, take the time *now* to get the phone numbers for emergency personnel in their areas. Get an old fashioned address book and put those numbers right under your loved one's names and addresses. You could save precious time if your grandparents start having medical issues while you're on the phone with them. Don't wait until Uncle John collapses on the other end of a long distance call to try

to get the police and fire department phone numbers three states away. Every second counts when a person can't breathe!

3. Make a simple sketch of your street, noting the actual street addresses of neighboring houses. That way, if an emergency arises, the responding police and/or fire personnel will have an actual address to respond to, and won't have to rely on vague directions. And please make sure your own house numbers are clearly visible from the street.

4. Keep your own address taped to the wall near the telephone, or in an easily accessible place. It will be useful for caregivers who may need to call for assistance.

5. If possible, install a flashing porch light to use in case of an emergency to help rescuers find your house more quickly at night. If there is more than one person in the house, assign each person a job to avoid panic. Even a young child could flick a porch light on and off to alert emergency personnel. Older children could be told to wait outside to wave down

rescuers. Don't force them watch the person in distress.
6. Remember, *you* are the eyes and ears until rescuers arrive. Give complete and truthful answers to questions asked by the dispatcher. Don't worry about "being embarrassed" because Johnny took an overdose of drugs. The lives and safety of your loved ones could very well depend on your ability to remain calm and give accurate information. Screaming and crying accomplishes nothing, but will cost precious minutes, which could result in their death.
7. When rescuers arrive, obey their orders and get out of their way. It is impossible to do CPR or extract a person who is trapped if you insist on throwing yourself between the rescuer and the victim. They know what they're doing, so don't interfere.
8. Take the time now to get phone numbers for plumbers, carpenters, A/C repairmen, etc., and keep them in one place. Don't tie up the 911 system for something stupid.
9. Teach your kids that 911 is an important tool. They should never be

allowed to dial 911 unless there is a real emergency. Not only does it waste time, because officers have to respond to every call, it could also result in citations and fines.
10. When in doubt, call 911. If you are feeling badly, call for help. Chest pains should never be ignored. Being stubborn could cost you your life. Use your head and live.

Together, 911 and the public can make an unbeatable team. Learn to use it properly and you will protect yourself, your family and you can save lives.

About the Author

Rhea Beth Compton spent many years as a 911 operator for various agencies in the metro Phoenix area. She kept a diary of her most unforgettable adventures and stories throughout her career, as evidenced by the stories in this book series. Though she is no longer in police work, she still strongly supports the police and respects the daily commitment that they show to public safety. She now occupies most of her time with her writing, in which she also helps other people achieve their dreams of being published. She currently resides in Glendale, Arizona with her son Jim, who is also an author, and a bunch of spoiled cats.

CPSIA information can be obtained
at www.ICGtesting.com
Printed in the USA
LVHW082203040421
683422LV00033B/1253